Grover Cleveland

The Presidents of the United States

George Washington
1789–1797

John Adams
1797–1801

Thomas Jefferson
1801–1809

James Madison
1809–1817

James Monroe
1817–1825

John Quincy Adams
1825–1829

Andrew Jackson
1829–1837

Martin Van Buren
1837–1841

William Henry Harrison
1841

John Tyler
1841–1845

James Polk
1845–1849

Zachary Taylor
1849–1850

Millard Fillmore
1850–1853

Franklin Pierce
1853–1857

James Buchanan
1857–1861

Abraham Lincoln
1861–1865

Andrew Johnson
1865–1869

Ulysses S. Grant
1869–1877

Rutherford B. Hayes
1877–1881

James Garfield
1881

Chester Arthur
1881–1885

Grover Cleveland
1885–1889

Benjamin Harrison
1889–1893

Grover Cleveland
1893–1897

William McKinley
1897–1901

Theodore Roosevelt
1901–1909

William H. Taft
1909–1913

Woodrow Wilson
1913–1921

Warren Harding
1921–1923

Calvin Coolidge
1923–1929

Herbert Hoover
1929–1933

Franklin D. Roosevelt
1933–1945

Harry Truman
1945–1953

Dwight Eisenhower
1953–1961

John F. Kennedy
1961–1963

Lyndon B. Johnson
1963–1969

Richard Nixon
1969–1974

Gerald Ford
1974–1977

Jimmy Carter
1977–1981

Ronald Reagan
1981–1989

George H. W. Bush
1989–1993

William J. Clinton
1993–2001

George W. Bush
2001–2009

Barack Obama
2009–

★ ★ ★ ★ ★ ★ ★ ★ ★ ★ ★ ★ ★ ★ ★ ★ ★ ★ ★

Presidents and Their Times

GROVER CLEVELAND

STEVEN OTFINOSKI

 **Marshall Cavendish**
Benchmark
New York

Website: www.marshallcavendish.us

This publication represents the opinions and views of the author based on Steven Otfinoski's personal experience, knowledge, and research. The information in this book serves as a general guide only. The author and publisher have used their best efforts in preparing this book and disclaim liability rising directly and indirectly from the use and application of this book.

Other Marshall Cavendish Offices:
Marshall Cavendish International (Asia) Private Limited, 1 New Industrial Road, Singapore 536196 • Marshall Cavendish International (Thailand) Co Ltd. 253 Asoke, 12th Flr, Sukhumvit 21 Road, Klongtoey Nua, Wattana, Bangkok 10110, Thailand • Marshall Cavendish (Malaysia) Sdn Bhd, Times Subang, Lot 46, Subang Hi-Tech Industrial Park, Batu Tiga, 40000 Shah Alam, Selangor Darul Ehsan, Malaysia

Marshall Cavendish is a trademark of Times Publishing Limited

All websites were available and accurate when this book was sent to press.

Library of Congress Cataloging-in-Publication Data

Otfinoski, Steven.
Grover Cleveland / by Steven Otfinoski.
p. cm. — (Presidents and their times)
Summary: "Provides comprehensive information on President Grover Cleveland and places him within his historical and cultural context. Also explored are the formative events of his times and how he responded"— Provided by publisher.
Includes bibliographical references and index.
ISBN 978-0-7614-4811-2
1.Cleveland, Grover, 1837–1908—Juvenile literature. 2. Presidents—United States—Biography—Juvenile literature. I. Title.
E697.O84 2011
973.8'5092—dc22
[B]
2009029689

Editor: Christine Florie
Publisher: Michelle Bisson
Art Director: Anahid Hamparian
Series Designer: Alex Ferrari

Photo research by Thomas Khoo

The photographs in this book are used by permission and through the courtesy of: *Corbis:* 16, 25, 61, 66, 67, 90; *Getty Images:* 20, 22, 55, 57, 63, 65; *North Wind Picture Archives:* 6, 7, 8, 9, 10, 14, 15, 27, 28, 36, 43, 47, 49, 51, 56, 68, 69, 73, 74, 75, 80, 86, 87, 96 (l), 97 (l); *Photolibrary:* 33, 38, 59, 71, 87, 92, 97 (r); *Topfoto:* cover, 3, 13, 23, 29, 30, 34, 44, 45, 48, 50, 52, 54, 62, 77, 78, 82, 85, 88, 95.

Printed in Malaysia
1 3 5 6 4 2

CONTENTS

$\mathcal{G}$rover Cleveland is one of the forgotten presidents of the United States. But Cleveland was one of our stronger presidents in an era when presidents were more caretakers of government than leaders of the nation. Cleveland had many of the qualities that people look to in a president: courage, empathy, and energy. He was a hardworking president. And the hard work paid off for him. He is the only U.S. president to serve two nonconsecutive terms. He served as both the nation's twenty-second and twenty-fourth president.

A DISTINGUISHED FAMILY

Stephen Grover Cleveland was born on March 18, 1837, in Caldwell, New Jersey. He was the fifth of nine children born to the Reverend Richard Falley Cleveland, a Presbyterian minister, and his wife, Ann Neal Cleveland. The family had only recently moved to New Jersey from Virginia, where Richard had previously been a pastor. In Caldwell, Richard took over a congregation from the Reverend Stephen Grover, a much-beloved pastor, for whom he named his third son.

Cleveland's father Richard was a Presbyterian minister.

Cleveland's birthplace, "The Manse," is located in Caldwell, New Jersey.

Although relatively poor, the Cleveland family had a distinguished ancestry. Moses Cleaveland (the first *a* in their last name was later dropped) arrived in the American colonies in 1634 as an apprentice to a **joiner**. His great-grandson, Aaron Cleaveland, was an Episcopalian minister and a friend of Benjamin Franklin. His son, also named Aaron, was a member of the Connecticut state legislature and introduced the first bill that called for the **abolition** of slavery in America. Another Moses Cleaveland, a surveyor, helped to establish a settlement on the south shore of Lake Erie in 1796. It was named Cleaveland in his honor. Cleveland, respelled in 1832, would grow to become the largest city in the state of Ohio.

Grover's mother, Ann, was originally from Baltimore, Maryland. Her father emigrated there from Ireland and was a bookseller and publisher. Her mother was a **Quaker** from Germantown, Pennsylvania. Richard and Ann met and married while he was a tutor in Baltimore before becoming a pastor.

In 1841, when Stephen was four, the family moved to the village of Fayetteville in western New York, where Richard took over a church. Stephen grew up in a strict but loving Christian home and from an early age was taught the values of honesty, humility, and hard work. "Often and often as a boy, I was compelled to get out of my warm bed at night, to hang up a hat or other garment which I had left on the floor," he said years later.

He was a big, strapping boy whom his friends called Big Steve. He didn't like his first name, however, and when he got a little older, he took his middle name, Grover, as his first name.

Cleveland attended Fayetteville Academy, where he was a good student but had to work hard at his studies. Learning didn't come easily for him. His favorite pastimes, when he wasn't studying or doing chores, were swimming and fishing. Fishing would become a lifelong passion.

This idyllic woodcut of a boy fishing, reflects only a part of Cleveland's childhood.

Young Grover worked for more than a year in a country store much like this one.

End of Childhood

When Cleveland was fourteen years old, the family moved to Clinton, New York, where his father took a better-paying position as district secretary of the American Home Missionary Society. Grover missed his friends back in Fayetteville and always looked back fondly on his years there. "[The benefits of living there] have gone with me in every step in life," he wrote years later.

He briefly attended the Clinton Liberal Institute but dropped out of school to go to work to help support his always-struggling family. He worked in a grocery store in Fayetteville as a clerk for one dollar a week, with room and board. After a year his pay was raised to two dollars a week. Seeing little future for himself in the grocery business, Grover returned to his parents' home in Clinton. Now age sixteen, he hoped to attend nearby Hamilton College, where his older brother William went to school. But then the family moved again to the village of Holland Patent in 1853. Within three weeks of arriving at his new church, Reverend Cleveland, who had been in poor health for years, died suddenly. All thoughts of college ended for Grover. He needed to work full-time now to help support his mother and sisters. He would be the last U.S. president except for Harry Truman not to have a college education.

William Cleveland, recently graduated from Hamilton College, was a teacher at the New York Institute for the Blind in New York City. He was able to get his younger brother Grover a job there as an assistant teacher. Grover taught reading, writing, arithmetic, and geography to the 116 students at the institute.

He also was the night supervisor in the boys' dormitory. Grover found the atmosphere depressing, however, and disliked the administrators' harsh treatment of the students. He left after a year and returned to Holland Patent.

On His Own

A wealthy neighbor and fellow Presbyterian, Ingham Townsend, took a liking to young Grover. He offered to pay for him to go to college if he would study to become a minister like his father. But Grover was more interested in the law than the ministry, and he turned down the offer. Instead, Townsend agreed to loan him twenty-five dollars to travel to Cleveland, the Ohio city founded by his ancestor, where he hoped to get a job in a law office.

On the way to Cleveland, Grover's train stopped in Buffalo, New York, where his mother's brother, Lewis W. Allen, lived. Grover decided to stay over in Buffalo and visit his uncle Lewis. Allen was impressed with Grover and persuaded him to stay on in Buffalo to pursue his ambitions. He offered him a job working on his farm, where he raised short-horned cattle. Grover worked on his uncle's farm and even helped Allen write a book about cattle raising. After about six months Allen used his influence to get his nephew a job as a clerk in the law firm of Rogers, Bowen and Rogers. In those days most law students did not study in college but clerked in law offices, where they could learn the profession while reading law books in their spare time. Cleveland approached his new job with characteristic energy.

In May 1859, at age twenty-two, Cleveland was admitted to the bar as a lawyer. Rogers, Bowen and Rogers hired him at a salary of one thousand dollars a year. Cleveland left his uncle's

Bustling Buffalo, City on the Lake

Cleveland's decision to pursue his ambitions in Buffalo was a good one. Established as a settlement in 1803 at the eastern end of Lake Erie, Buffalo began to grow quickly after the opening of the Erie Canal in 1825. The canal linked Buffalo with New York City. By 1860 Buffalo was a bustling city of more than 80,000 residents, roughly the same size as Chicago, Illinois. About 60 percent of the population were immigrants from Ireland and Germany who worked on the docks and in the mills. Buffalo was a busy port, with boatloads of goods traveling west to Chicago and east to New York City. By 1900 the city was an industrial giant with a population of 352,000. The following year the Pan-American Exposition made Buffalo world famous. The fair promoted good relations between North and South America. It ended in tragedy, however, on September 6, 1901, when President William McKinley was shot by an assassin at the exposition's Temple of Music and died eight days later.

house and moved to downtown Buffalo, where he then worked. He lived in a series of boardinghouses and hotels. Cleveland was a workhorse in the law office and a skillful litigator in the courtroom. His arguments were always sound, and he knew his cases thoroughly.

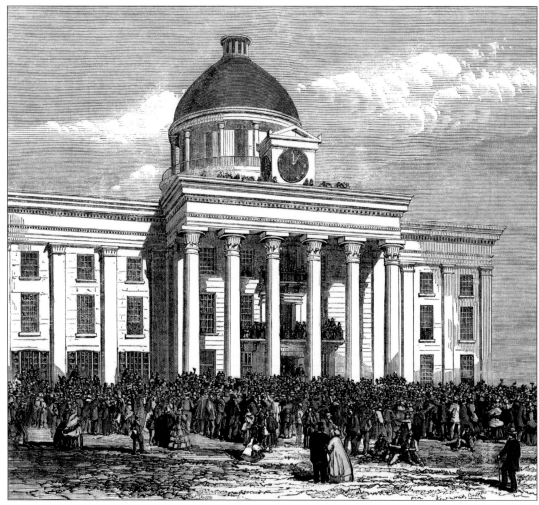

Jefferson Davis is inaugurated as president of the Confederate States in Montgomery, Alabama, in February 1861, two months before the outbreak of the Civil War.

The Civil War

In April 1861 the growing conflict between the federal government and the Southern states over slavery and states' rights erupted into war. Between December 1860 and March 1861, seven Southern states had **seceded** from the United States and formed their own **confederacy**, naming Jefferson Davis their president. Four more states later joined the Confederacy. The Northern states that remained in the Union

This elaborate banner commemorates the Secession Convention held at Charleston, South Carolina, in 1861. South Carolina was the first state to secede from the Union.

were under the leadership of the recently elected **Republican** president Abraham Lincoln.

As an able-bodied, unmarried man, Cleveland may have been expected to sign up to fight for the Union in the Civil War. But as a member of the **Democratic Party**, he opposed the war, feeling the Southern states had a right to leave the Union if they chose to. He also felt his income was needed to support his mother and sisters. His brothers Fred and Cecil volunteered to serve. Both of them survived the war.

Horatio Seymour, elected governor of New York for the second time in 1862, became Cleveland's first political patron.

Meanwhile, Cleveland began to pursue an interest in politics. In 1862 he was elected Democratic supervisor of his city **ward** and was a campaign worker for the Democratic candidate for governor, Horatio Seymour, speaker of the New York House of Representatives. When Seymour won the governorship, he rewarded Cleveland, then twenty-eight years old, with an appointment as assistant district attorney of Erie County. In this position Cleveland helped District Attorney C. C. Torrance handle law cases for the county government. Cleveland proved so good at his job that Torrance, who lived outside Buffalo, let him do most of his day-to-day work.

As the war wore on, more soldiers were needed on the front line. A national **draft** was put into force in 1863, and Cleveland was called to serve. Still the main financial supporter of his mother and sisters, Cleveland decided to take the legal way out of serving and hired a substitute. For $150, George Benninsky, a thirty-two-year-old Polish immigrant, agreed to take Cleveland's place as a Union solider. He served faithfully and survived the war.

The Use of Substitutes in the Civil War

The practice of hiring someone to serve in one's place in the Civil War was common and legal in the North by 1862. Up until February 1864, a man who wanted to avoid serving had the choice of hiring a substitute or paying the government three hundred dollars. After that, substitutes were the only option; and with every subsequent draft, a man could be liable to serve again and had to hire another substitute. Only the well-to-do could afford to avoid service this way, making the system unfair to those in the lower classes. The Southern Confederacy also allowed substitutes but abolished the practice by the end of 1863 as the number of eligible men available to serve dwindled.

A Career in Politics

The war ended in Union victory in April 1865. That same year the twenty-eight-year-old Cleveland made his first attempt to gain elected office. He ran as the Democratic candidate for district attorney of Erie County. The county was heavily Republican, but Cleveland made a good showing. He lost to his friend Lyman K. Bass in a surprisingly close race. Cleveland returned to his law practice, which flourished more than ever.

In 1870 he was approached by local Democrats, who admired him for his honesty and hard work, to run for office again, this time for the position of county sheriff. It was a job that might seem too humble for a successful lawyer, but Cleveland accepted

GROVER CLEVELAND, HANGMAN

One of the duties of the sheriff in Erie County was to preside over the public executions of condemned criminals. Previous sheriffs had turned over this distasteful job of hangman to subordinates or hired people. But Cleveland felt he should not give any duty to someone else that he was not willing to do himself. When the time came on September 6, 1872, for Patrick Morrissey, convicted of murdering his mother, to be hanged, Cleveland lived up to his words. At noon, standing 20 feet from the condemned man, he pushed the lever that dropped the gallows trap and hanged Morrissey. While Cleveland was resolute in performing his duty, he was not unfeeling. According to a 1912 article published in *The New York Times*, "[a] few Buffalo people still live who can bear out the statement that this little tragedy made Mr. Cleveland a sick man for several days thereafter."

the nomination. He may have wanted the job of sheriff for economic reasons. The sheriff received a good salary and could augment it with fees for various jobs he performed for the public. Cleveland needed the money to help support his family. He also looked to the shorter hours as a welcome break from his long hours in his law practice. He won the election by just 303 votes.

Cleveland fulfilled his duties as sheriff with characteristic thoroughness. He also maintained strict honesty and was intolerant of corruption. When he found out that politicians who provided the county jail with food and fuel were cheating by falling short on their orders, he quickly put a stop to it.

After his term as sheriff ended in 1873, Cleveland returned to his law practice. He had saved $20,000 while sheriff, allowing him to be debt-free for the first time in his career. As his law practice grew, so did his bank account.

A confirmed bachelor now in his mid-thirties, Cleveland enjoyed the city's nightlife, making the rounds of German restaurants and city saloons with his colleagues. He enjoyed the lively political talk and fellowship as much as the glasses of beer and good food that he consumed. Always large in size, Cleveland was now developing a sizable waistline. His many nieces and nephews affectionately referred to him as Uncle Jumbo.

Much of the talk in the taverns was about the corruption in politics. Like many American cities of the day, Buffalo was riddled with crooked politicians, both Democrats and Republicans. The public was tired of the **kickbacks** politicians took from contracts for services and for the promotion to office of party hacks for their loyalty and not their competence. Reform-minded Democrats were looking for a candidate for the mayoral election of 1881. They decided that Grover Cleveland, whose reputation for honesty had been established both in the sheriff's office and in the law courts, was the man for the job. After some initial reluctance, Cleveland agreed to run for mayor. Thus began one of the swiftest rises in the history of American politics that in three short years would take Cleveland from the mayor's mansion in Buffalo to the White House in Washington, D.C.

$\mathcal{O}$hio senator James A. Garfield won the 1880 presidential election, becoming the fifth Republican president in a row. But in New York State the Democrats made impressive gains in state and local elections that year. New Yorkers were tired of Republican control of the government and the corruption it brought,

Presidential candidate James Garfield and his running mate Chester Arthur are depicted in this Republican banner of 1880. Garfield won, but died from an assassin's bullet only six months into his term.

although Democrats, especially the politicians who ran New York City's Tammany Hall, were just as corrupt.

Grover Cleveland, independent and honest, was seen by many people as a sign of hope in Buffalo politics. In the November 1881 mayoral election he won with 15,120 votes to Republican candidate Milton C. Beebe's 11,528 votes. Cleveland took office on January 2, 1882, vowing to clean up city government and serve the people's interests.

THE VETO MAYOR

As mayor, Cleveland fulfilled his promise of reform. He **vetoed** any bill crossing his desk that included wasteful spending or smelled of **graft** or kickbacks to the lawmakers who proposed it. One street-cleaning contract bill was to go to the highest bidder because the company was friendly with members of the city council. Cleveland vetoed it and retorted, "I regard it as the culmination of a most bare-faced, impudent, and shameless scheme to betray the interests of the people, and to worse than squander the public money." The contract went to the lowest bidder.

The Veto Mayor, as he came to be called, ended up saving the city more than a million dollars in just one year. However, Cleveland could take positive action when it was called for, too. A city canal was infested with sewage that seeped into private wells, contaminating drinking water. Some of the residents who drank the polluted water came down with typhoid, cholera, or other diseases. In the year 1881 more than 1,300 deaths were attributed to these water-borne illnesses. The city council wanted to appoint a task force of local politicians to deal with the matter, but Cleveland said no. Instead, he brought in an outside team of engineers who cleaned up the pollution and established a new sewage system.

Tammany Hall

Tammany Hall, for much of its infamous history, was as much a state of mind as a place. The Society of Tammany was founded in New York City on May 12, 1789, as a fraternal organization whose members met to socialize and promote the rights of middle-class residents. It was named for Tammany an early Delaware Indian chief known for his wisdom. Within fifteen years Tammany members formed a majority in the New York City Democratic Party Committee.

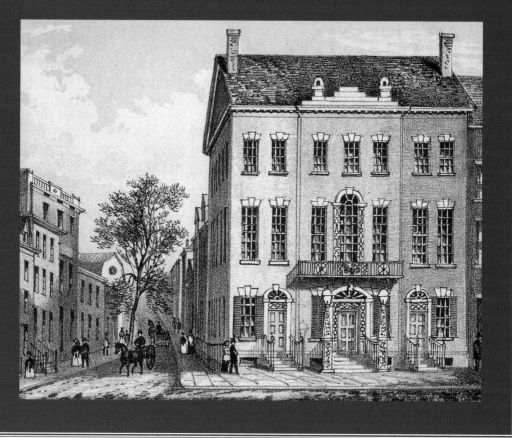

By mid-century, Tammany was a powerful force in state and city politics. Tammany Hall (left), the organization's headquarters on Madison Avenue in New York City, became synonymous with corruption when Tammany boss William Marcy Tweed (right) was arrested and convicted of graft in 1871. Tammany regained power in 1886 under the leadership of Robert Croaker. It continued to run politics in New York City until its power was broken in 1932, when Tammany mayor Jimmy Walker was forced to resign amid charges of corruption. A new era of reform was ushered in with the election of Mayor Fiorello LaGuardia.

"Good and pure government lies at the foundation of the wealth and progress of every community," Cleveland declared at a cornerstone-laying ceremony for a Young Men's Christian Association building. At the Democratic State Convention to nominate a candidate for governor in September 1882, some delegates supported Cleveland. They thought his honest, reform brand of government could be applied not just to a community, but to the entire state. Two other candidates, Roswell P. Flower and Henry W. Slocum, led in voting on the first **ballot** but were in a deadlock. Cleveland soon emerged as a compromise candidate and won the nomination. While popular in Buffalo, Cleveland was little known outside of western New York. Nevertheless, the corrupt leaders of Tammany Hall gave him their support, thinking that if he won the governorship, they would be able to control him.

The state Republicans enjoyed no such unity. The party's candidate for governor was Charles J. Folger, former secretary of the Treasury in the administration of President Chester Arthur, who succeeded President Garfield after he was assassinated in 1881. Folger was the candidate of the rich and powerful, and many reform-minded Republicans crossed party lines to vote for Cleveland.

On election day in November 1882, Cleveland won with 535,318 votes to Folger's 342,464. It was the largest plurality of votes in a New York gubernatorial election up to that time. The Democrats also won a majority in the state assembly. Cleveland's beloved mother did not live to see her son's victory. She died almost four months earlier, at age seventy-eight.

A POPULAR GOVERNOR

On a snowy New Year's Day in 1883, the forty-six-year-old Cleveland delivered a heartfelt inaugural address without notes—long his practice as a lawyer in courtrooms. "The interests now transferred to new hands are yours," he declared to the people of

New York, "and the duties here newly assumed should be performed for your benefit and your good."

Cleveland's speech may have been uninspired, but the sentiment behind it was genuine. He was totally committed to his job of governor. Unmarried, without a family to attend to, he spent nearly every waking moment working. Before signing, or more often vetoing, a bill, he would read every word of it, often working late into the night. His office door was always open to visitors and those seeking political appointments, but he gave no favors to party members based solely on their loyalty. This angered the leaders of Tammany Hall, who could see at that point that they would never control the Veto Governor.

This celebratory scene took place after Cleveland was elected governor of New York.

Cleveland played no favorites. When a bill came in from his hometown of Fayetteville requesting a loan to buy a new steam fire engine, he vetoed it. He also vetoed a bill to lower streetcar fares in New York City. According to Cleveland, the reduction violated the terms of a previous transportation contact.

While he was quick to veto, he was often slow to take action. In Cleveland's philosophy, government should intervene in public affairs only to maintain law and order and to protect property rights. But there were exceptions. As a fisherman and outdoorsman, he valued the natural environment. When the region that encompassed Niagara Falls in upstate New York was threatened by industrial development, he moved to make the area into a 1.5-million-acre park. He also prohibited child labor and supported improvements in the state educational system. For these achievements, New Yorkers dubbed him Grover the Good.

THE ELECTION OF 1884

Cleveland's term as governor made him a national figure. He had become the rising star of the Democratic Party. When Democrats met in Chicago in July 1884 to nominate a candidate for president, Cleveland was the natural choice. His independence and reform politics were balanced by his conservative views of government's role in society. On the second ballot of the convention Cleveland easily gained enough votes for the nomination. Governor Thomas A. Hendricks of Indiana, eighteen years older than Cleveland, was chosen as his running mate to satisfy the party's Old Guard.

At their convention in Chicago in June, the Republicans nominated James G. Blaine of Maine for president. Blaine was the

This woodcut shows New York's Governor Cleveland signing a reform bill as Police Commissioner Theodore Roosevelt looks on approvingly.

The Democratic Convention in Chicago nominated Cleveland for president in 1884.

most popular Republican of his time, but also one of the most controversial. He had vied for his party's presidential nomination in 1880, but revelations of crooked dealings with the railroad companies destroyed his chances. Now he was back running again and was determined to win.

The reformers in the Republican Party were appalled at Blaine's nomination. Many became what were called **Mugwumps**, an Algonquin Indian word for *chiefs*, and crossed party lines to support Cleveland's candidacy.

The 1884 campaign was not a high point in presidential elections. There were few important issues at stake, and the campaign turned into a mudslinging contest between the two candidates. While Blaine was seen as questionable in his public life, Cleveland was attacked for supposed sins in his private life. On July 2 the *Buffalo Evening Telegraph* broke a story that eleven years earlier Cleveland had seduced a young widow named Maria Halpin and had an illegitimate child with her. It accused Cleveland of locking up Halpin and his son to save his career. A source of these rumors was a Buffalo clergyman, the Reverend George H. Ball, who claimed Halpin was not the first or last of Cleveland's conquests.

Cleveland and his running mate Thomas A. Hendricks posed for this presidential campaign poster.

CLEVELAND'S FIRST VICE PRESIDENT

Thomas Hendricks had a distinguished career in politics before he became vice president. He was born in Ohio in 1819 but was raised in Indiana, where his uncle served as governor from 1822 to 1825. Hendricks became a lawyer in 1843 and, after serving in the Indiana state legislature, was elected to the

U.S. House of Representatives in 1851. He later ran for governor of his state but lost and was elected to the U.S. Senate in 1863. An influential Democratic senator, Hendricks led the defense of President Andrew Johnson, whose sympathies for the defeated South brought charges of impeachment against him from Northern Republicans who wanted to make the Southern states suffer for their secession from the Union. Hendricks and other Democratic senators saved Johnson from the indignity of being convicted and removed from office.

After leaving the Senate, Hendricks ran again for governor of Indiana and won. He became the first Democratic governor elected in the North after the Civil War. In 1876 he ran for vice president on a ticket with Samuel J. Tilden, who lost to Republican Rutherford B. Hayes in a close and controversial election. Hendricks was luckier in his second try for vice president with Cleveland. He filled an office that had been vacant since Vice President Chester Arthur became president in 1881. Hendricks's tenure, however, would be brief. Five months after assuming office, on November 25, 1885, he died in his sleep during a trip home to Indiana. No one would fill the office of vice president until Levi Morton, who served in that capacity after his running mate, Benjamin Harrison, was elected president in 1889.

"Women now married and anxious to cover the sins of their youth have been his victims, and are now alarmed lest their relations with him shall be exposed." When his campaign manager asked Cleveland how they should respond to the charges, the candidate replied, "Tell the truth."

Cleveland did not deny his relationship with Halpin nor that he supported her child, although he did not acknowledge that the boy was his. The Republicans gleefully made a campaign slogan of the scandal:

"Ma, ma, where's my Pa?
Gone to the White House, ha, ha, ha!"

Cleveland and the Widow Halpin

The full truth about Cleveland's relationship with Maria Halpin may never be known, but it is clear that the tabloid version spread during the 1884 campaign was filled with untruths. Halpin, a thirty-three-year-old widow, moved to Buffalo from Jersey City, New Jersey, in 1871, leaving two children behind. She found a job in a dry goods store and became a popular figure in her community. She had an affair not only with Cleveland, who was a year older than she was, but with other men in his social circle, including possibly his good friend and law partner Oscar Folsom. When Halpin had her child in 1874, she named the boy Oscar Folsom Cleveland. She may have named Cleveland as the father of her child because he was a bachelor and was free to marry her. Cleveland, however, learning of her other affairs, broke off the relationship but agreed to assume responsibility for her child. He may have done so to protect Folsom, who was married.

Halpin began drinking heavily and neglected little Oscar. Cleveland, through a friend who was a judge, had her committed to an asylum and the child put in an orphanage. Later he persuaded Halpin to leave Buffalo and helped set her up in business in Niagara Falls. She returned in 1876 and, denied custody of the child, kidnapped him. Oscar was later returned, and Halpin disappeared. She resurfaced during Cleveland's second term as president, writing him for money.

The Halpin relationship did not have long-term effects on Cleveland's presidency. Yet it hurt him deeply that a Buffalo newspaper and local residents had led the attack against him. He rarely returned to the city where he got his start after that.

This 1884 magazine cover cartoon attacks the Democratic candidate who allegedly fathered a child out of wedlock years earlier. The cartoon is satirically entitled "Another Vote for Cleveland."

The Democrats responded by spreading a rumor that Blaine, the solid family man, had his first son less than three months after marrying his wife. Cleveland refused to support this attack, but that didn't stop his supporters from coming up with their own little ditty about the Republican candidate and his questionable record in office:

"Blaine! Blaine! James G. Blaine!
Continental liar from the State of Maine!"

The attacks on Cleveland's character hurt him in the polls, and as Election Day approached, Blaine's chances of winning looked very good. His home state of Maine voted early and gave Blaine the largest Republican victory ever.

Unlike Cleveland, who did little campaigning, Blaine made a six-week sweep of the country, giving four hundred speeches. Six days before the election, Blaine was scheduled to speak in New York City, confident that he could win Cleveland's home state, which had the most **electoral votes**. Before his speech, Presbyterian minister Samuel D. Burchard addressed the crowd. "We are Republicans," said Burchard, "and don't propose to leave our party and identify ourselves with the party whose antecedents have been Rum, Romanism, and Rebellion." The

Republican James G. Blaine was one of his party's best-known leaders in the post-Civil War era.

rebellion referred to the Civil War and the Southern Democrats who defied the Union. Romanism referred to Roman Catholicism, the religion of Irish Democrats.

The quotation was picked up by reporters who were present and made the front page of Democratic newspapers. Blaine, in his defense, was waiting to speak and probably didn't even hear what Burchard had said; but he was now branded, fairly or not, as being anti-Catholic. He later disavowed himself of the comments, but the damage had already been done. That evening Blaine added to the problems he faced with middle- and lower-class New Yorkers by attending a fund-raising dinner at Delmonico's restaurant with some of the state's wealthiest men, including Jay Gould and John Jacob Astor. On election day Blaine lost New York State by 1,149 votes, and Cleveland won the national electoral vote, 219 to 182. However, he squeaked by in the **popular vote**, with only 23,000 more votes than Blaine. Forty-seven-year-old Grover Cleveland had become the first Democratic president to be elected since James Buchanan, twenty-eight years earlier.

Democrats turned the Republican's anti-Cleveland ditty into a song of triumph:

"Hurrah for Maria! Hurrah for the kid!
I voted for Cleveland, and I'm damned glad I did!

Cleveland's inauguration in 1885 brought the Democrats back into the White House for the first time in twenty-eight years.

GROVER THE GOOD Three

On March 4, 1885, Grover Cleveland delivered his fifteen-minute inaugural address from memory. "To-day the executive branch of the Government is transferred to new keeping," he told the assembled crowd.

> But this is still the Government of all the people, and it should be none the less an object of their affectionate solicitude. At this hour the animosities of political strife, the bitterness of partisan defeat, and the exultation of partisan triumph should be supplanted by an ungrudging acquiescence in the popular will and a sober, conscientious concern for the general weal [welfare]. Moreover, if from this hour we cheerfully and honestly abandon all sectional prejudice and distrust, and determine, with manly confidence in one another, to work out harmoniously the achievements of our national destiny, we shall deserve to realize all the benefits which our happy form of government can bestow.

Cleveland came to the presidency with no clear plan or program, but for most Americans this was not a concern. The Civil War was over, and Reconstruction had ended some years before. Americans were ready to get back to the job of building their nation and achieving prosperity. It was enough to have a man in charge who was honest, dependable, and watching out for the public welfare.

Cleveland chose men for his cabinet who represented the different sections of the country. They included a brilliant and thoughtful scholar (Secretary of State Thomas F. Bayard of Delaware), a conservative Republican (Secretary of War William Crowninshield Endicott of Massachusetts), a youthful Westerner (Postmaster General William F. Vilas of Wisconsin), and two Southerners, both of whom had served in the Confederacy (Attorney General Augustus H. Garland of Arkansas and Secretary of the Interior Lucius Q. C. Lamar of Mississippi).

President Cleveland (third from right) poses with his cabinet. Vice President Hendricks sits across from Cleveland.

The Issue of Patronage

Every new president is beleaguered by people wanting government jobs. Cleveland had campaigned that he would continue the reform of the patronage system begun years earlier by President Rutherford B. Hayes and his Republican successors in the White House. Under this patronage, or spoils system, the winning party gave government jobs to its members, rewarding them for their loyalty, whether they had the skills or experience necessary for the position. Under the reformers, jobs were not to go to party loyalists but to people who were qualified and competent, regardless of their political affiliation. Cleveland promised that he would divide the jobs equally between worthy Democrats and Republicans. But he found carrying out this reform to be difficult. Democrats had been out of power in Washington for a quarter century and demanded their opportunity to work in his administration. Cleveland, despite good intentions, found himself obliged to replace many Republicans in office with Democrats simply because they belonged to his party. Many Mugwump Republicans who had supported Cleveland were unhappy and disillusioned with the new president. Feeling the pressure from both sides, Cleveland exclaimed in frustration, "My God, what is there in this office that any man should ever want to get into it!"

The Veto President

The Civil War had been over for two decades, but many of the men who had fought in it were still alive. When Cleveland took office, there were about 900,000 pension claims filed by war veterans. Many of these claims were legitimate and based on wounds suffered in battle, but many others were not. If, for example, a veteran fell off a ladder while fixing his roof, he might make a claim. Previously, these claims were put through with a rubber stamp, but Cleveland vetoed hundreds of them as fraudulent. This angered powerful veterans organizations such as the Grand Army of the Republic (GAR), which represented Union veterans.

To stop Cleveland's vetoes, the GAR pushed the Dependent Pension Bill of 1887 through Congress. The bill would grant pensions to all disabled veterans, whether they were disabled in military service or not. Cleveland predictably vetoed the bill, but it passed three years later during the administration of Benjamin Harrison.

However, Cleveland was sensitive to other war wounds. He ordered the return of captured Confederate flags and banners to the Southern states from which they were taken. This caused an uproar among Union veterans and their supporters. "May God palsy [paralyze] the hand that wrote that order. May God palsy the brain that conceived it; and may God palsy the tongue that dictated it," declared GAR commander Lucius Fairchild, a hero of the Battle of Gettysburg. Cleveland quickly rescinded the order.

Cleveland's nickname, the Veto President, was well earned. In his first term alone Cleveland issued more than three hundred vetoes. All twenty-one previous presidents issued only 132 vetoes combined. Cleveland's decision to limit government spending and cut waste and graft was admirable. But there was little attempt on his part to actively shape policies that would have a more positive effect. His philosophy of government is summed up in the statement "Though the people support the Government, the Government should not support the people."

When Congress passed a bill to give Texas farmers ten thousand dollars for seed grain after their crops were destroyed by drought, Cleveland vetoed it. He wrote, "Federal aid in such cases encourages the expectation of paternal care on the part of the Government and weakens the sturdiness of our national character."

TAKING ON THE TARIFF AND SILVER CURRENCY

If there was a central issue in Cleveland's first term, it was the high **tariff** imposed on imported goods sold in the United States. Republican businessmen and industrialists favored a high tariff to protect their interests and discourage foreign competition in the marketplace. Cleveland felt the high tariff hurt the American consumer by keeping the prices of goods high, and that it would eventually lead to a damaging trade imbalance. He also saw the $70 million surplus the tariff brought into the Treasury as a source of temptation for congressmen and senators who dreamed up wasteful ways to spend it.

In his annual address to Congress in December 1887, Cleveland focused solely on one subject: the tariff—something no president had previously done. In July 1888 Congress passed the Mills Bill, which did slightly lower the tariff, but not enough for Cleveland's liking.

The farmers of the South and West supported Cleveland's stand. They believed a lower tariff would provide them with lower-priced, affordable imported goods. However, on the matter of currency, the farmers and the president did not agree. The farmers favored silver money that was cheap, would lower the price of goods, and would help them get out of debt.

Cleveland favored the continuation of the gold standard, whereby all currency was backed by gold stored in the U.S. Treasury. The Bland-Allison Act of 1878 required that the U.S. Treasury coin no less than $2 million of silver money a month. Putting more silver into circulation lowered the value of U.S. money. Some people used their silver to buy gold from the Treasury in limited amounts, a legal practice at the time. Other people hoarded gold, making it scarcer. Gold was slowly being drained from the Treasury, a situation the president believed would cause the economy to falter. Cleveland asked Congress to repeal the Bland-Allison Act and stop the steady flow of silver money. Congress refused to do so. The silver-gold debate would continue between Congress and the president for years to come.

LABOR AND LAND

As the power and influence of business and industry grew in America, the rights of workers became an issue. Trade or labor unions were formed to protect their rights, which were often neglected by their employers. One of the most important of these trade unions was the Knights of Labor, which organized workers to strike for higher wages and better working conditions. President Cleveland recognized the importance of labor and was the first president to devote an entire message to Congress on the subject. In April 1886 he called for Congress to establish a three-member commission to help arbitrate labor-management conflicts. Just two weeks later the Knights of Labor held a rally in downtown Chicago for striking factory workers. Police lined Haymarket Square, ready to break up the rally at the first sign of violence. Suddenly a bomb was thrown by an unknown person at the line of police. Seven officers were killed and fifty more injured. The so-called Haymarket Riot turned millions of American against the trade unions because they saw them as the tools of **anarchists**. Cleveland's call for a commission went unheeded. It took two years before he and Congress agreed on the establishment of a national Department of Labor.

The president was as concerned about the welfare of western homesteaders as he was about laborers. The wealthy railroad companies had taken over millions of acres in the West through

The bombing during the Haymarket Square riot in Chicago shocked the nation and tarnished the image of trade unions for many Americans.

government channels. Cleveland saw this as illegal and took back 81,000,000 acres of this land, opening it to homesteaders. He was not, however, insensitive to the rights of American Indians. Many of them had been herded from their original homes into a region called Indian Territory, later to become the state of Oklahoma. Before leaving office, President Chester Arthur had agreed to open Indian Territory to white settlement. Cleveland reversed that order and closed the territory to settlers, warning that anyone who disobeyed the law and entered Indian Territory would be forcibly removed by the military.

President Cleveland fought to protect Indian encampments like this one in Oklahoma Indian territory from white settlement.

Geronimo, the Last Warrior

Although Cleveland wanted to help American Indians retain their homelands, he had little patience for renegades who attacked soldiers and settlers. In the 1870s and 1880s the Chiricahua Apache, under their leader Geronimo, spread fear and terror among settlers in the Southwest. Several times Geronimo, whose name means "Jerome" in Spanish, agreed to settle on a reservation and then fled with his warriors to Mexico. Finally, after Geronimo's last

escape in 1885, Cleveland ordered American troops under General Nelson A. Miles to hunt him down. With only 35 warriors and 101 women and children, Geronimo led more than 5,000 soldiers on a long chase that finally ended with the Apaches' surrender in September 1886, effectively ending the Indian Wars in the West. The Apaches were sent to Florida and later returned west to a reservation at Fort Sill, Oklahoma, where Geronimo lived out his life. He earned money by appearing at fairs and exhibitions, where he would sign his autograph and pose for photographs. One night in 1909, while returning to Fort Sill on horseback, the eighty-year-old Geronimo fell off his horse and spent the night on the cold ground. He developed pneumonia and died soon after.

A WHITE HOUSE WEDDING

Grover Cleveland entered the White House a bachelor. The duties of White House hostess fell to his unmarried sister Rose, who was a former private school teacher and an outspoken feminist. She brought culture and new ideas to the White House but wasn't entirely happy about some of her duties as hostess. It is said that while shaking hands on long reception lines she would stave off boredom by conjugating Greek verbs to herself. Rose later wrote a book, *George Eliot's Poetry, and Other Studies,* which became a best seller. She attributed its success not to its content but to her celebrity as sister to the president.

Years earlier, Cleveland had become the executor of the estate of his good friend Oscar Folsom, who died in a carriage accident in 1875. He watched over the affairs of Folsom's widow and eleven-year-old daughter, Frances, who called him Uncle Cleve. As Frances, also known as Frank, grew into a beautiful young woman, Cleveland fell in love with her. She returned his affection, and by the time Cleveland was running for president, they were secretly engaged. After Frances returned from a year's grand tour of Europe with her mother, the president announced their engagement to a surprised nation. He was forty-nine and she, twenty-one. Their wedding took place on June 2, 1886, in the Blue Room of the White House before thirty-one invited guests. The pretty bride wore a white satin gown with a 15-foot train and a diamond necklace given to her by the groom. Composer and conductor John Philip Sousa led the U.S. Marine Band in "The Wedding March" from Wagner's opera *Lohengrin.* The Reverend William Cleveland, the president's brother, gave the benediction. The groom was so nervous that he forgot to kiss the bride after the ceremony.

While President John Tyler, a widower, married his second wife during his presidency, in 1844, Cleveland is the only president to be married in the White House. When asked by someone why he hadn't married before, Cleveland replied, only half jokingly, "I was waiting for my wife to grow up."

Marriage softened the rough edges of the often gruff Grover Cleveland. He was a doting husband and was happily surprised to find that his young wife was more socially adept than he was. She was a charming First Lady who improved her husband's popularity with the public.

The president and Frances Folsom's wedding in the White House's "Blue Room" was the social highlight of the year and a presidential first.

FRANCES FOLSOM CLEVELAND

Frances Cleveland was the youngest First Lady and, in her time, one of the most popular. She was born on July 21, 1864, in Buffalo. Despite her youth when she married, she was a charming and gracious First Lady. She held receptions for ladies three times a week, including one on Saturday afternoons for working girls. Later, when she had children, she created a kindergarten for them and her friends' children. She played piano, grew flowers, and was a respectable amateur photographer. The public adored her, and when she refused to wear a bustle—padding that puffed out the back of a woman's skirt—millions of American women followed suit.

After her husband's death in 1908, Frances continued to live in their retirement home in Princeton, New Jersey. In 1913 she married Thomas J. Preston Jr., a professor of archaeology at Princeton University. She remained a popular figure on the Princeton campus until her death at age eighty-four on October 29, 1947.

Perhaps the finest tribute to Frances as a mother was given by her daughter Marion, who once said, "My mother did not want us to grow up dwelling on the fact that we had been White House children. She trained us for living on our own account."

The press's stalking of the First Couple, however, infuriated Cleveland. On the first morning of their honeymoon he left his cabin in Maryland to find a mass of reporters waiting for him. His disdain for journalists went back to the campaign and the Halpin affair, and he was the last president to deny the White House press working space. They had to stand outside the White House and hope to snag an impromptu interview with visitors coming and going.

A Meager Social Life

Marriage did little to alter Cleveland's work habits. He continued to work late and was up at six in the morning and at his

In the White House, President Cleveland was a tireless worker as can be seen in this picture.

desk by eight. He went to work earlier during the summer. Cleveland wrote all his own speeches and sometimes even answered the White House telephone himself. His only daily breaks were a stroll or an afternoon carriage ride. He still enjoyed an occasional fishing expedition or a duck hunt with his trusty rifle, which he called Death and Destruction. Yet Cleveland refused to take rides on the presidential yacht. He was an avid baseball fan; but when the manager of the Chicago White Stockings invited him to a game, he declined, saying, "What do you think the American people would think of me if I wasted my time going to a baseball game?"

THE INTERSTATE COMMERCE ACT

Cleveland's differences with the railroads led to perhaps the most important bill of his first term. He had already forced the

Uncle Sam looks on as a group of cowboy Congressmen prepare to lassos the untamed railroads in this cartoon commemorating the creation of the Interstate Commerce Commission.

Railroads were the lifeblood of American commerce by the 1890s, when this woodcut of a New York City freight yard was made.

railroads to give back land that wasn't theirs. Now he wanted to make them lower their freight rates, which they set arbitrarily high. Congress passed, and the president signed, the Interstate Commerce Act in 1887, the first law that set regulations for the railroads. It led to the creation of the Interstate Commerce Commission (ICC), a regulatory agency that saw that railroad freight rates for interstate travel were fair and equitable. The first federal agency of its kind, the ICC set the pattern for many future regulatory agencies that protected the rights of private citizens with regard to private enterprise.

LADY LIBERTY

One of President Cleveland's grandest moments was presiding over the unveiling of the Statue of Liberty on Bedloe's Island (now Liberty Island) in New York Harbor on October 28, 1886. Ironically, Cleveland, while governor of New York, had vetoed a $50,000 expenditure for a pedestal for the statue, charging that since the statue was a gift from France to America, the government should not have to  assume the cost of the pedestal. Private donations ended up paying for the pedestal.

Among the invited guests was French sculptor Frédéric-Auguste Bartholdi, who had created the statue, officially named *Liberty Enlightening the World*. However, absent was Emma Lazarus, whose poem "The New Colossus" honored the statue and would be inscribed on a wall inside the pedestal in 1903. No women, in fact, were invited to the ceremony. This led a boatful of suffragettes to crash the ceremony and point out to the gathered men that Liberty was, after all, a lady.

Fog and light rain dampened the spirits of some and made Lady Liberty barely visible for many. But Cleveland was upbeat in his speech, declaring that "a stream of light shall pierce the darkness of ignorance and men's oppression until liberty shall enlighten the world."

As the presidential election year of 1888 approached, Cleveland's enemies had grown in number. Conservative Republicans were unhappy with his partial reform of the patronage system. Some Democrats and Mugwump Republicans were disappointed that he hadn't gone far enough in ending patronage. Big business was upset with him for his attacks on the tariff. The Republicans saw a chance to win back the White House, which they had lost four years earlier.

$\mathcal{A}$s an **incumbent** president, Cleveland had little trouble obtaining his party's nomination when the Democrats convened in St. Louis, Missouri, in June 1888. Former Ohio senator Allen Granby Thurman, seventy-five years old, was chosen as Cleveland's running mate even though he opposed the president on several important issues, including lowering the tariff.

Cleveland and running mate Allen G. Thurman are presented by an approving, if somewhat relaxed, Uncle Sam in this campaign poster from the 1888 presidential election.

The Republican convention held the same month in Chicago had several powerful men vying for the nomination, including former Ohio senator John Sherman and Chauncey M. Depew, a brilliant orator and director of Cornelius Vanderbilt's railroads. Former Indiana senator Benjamin Harrison was at the back of the pack in the early voting but proved a **dark horse**, winning the nomination on the eighth **ballot**. Harrison, fifty-four, seemed a curious choice. Although he had few enemies, he was aloof and was considered, even by his friends, to be a cold fish. Standing only 5 feet 6 inches tall, Harrison was a bit of a dandy who sported a beaver hat and was called "Kid Glove" Harrison. His strong points were his Civil War record—he was promoted to **brevet** general by war's end—and his family background. His great-grandfather, another Benjamin Harrison, was a signer of the Declaration of Independence; and his grandfather was William Henry Harrison, the ninth president. Levi Morton, a New York banker and one of the richest men in America, was chosen as Harrison's running mate.

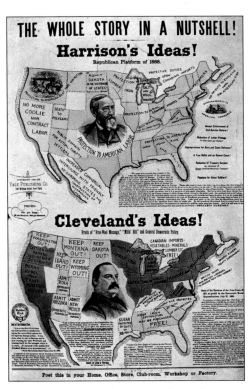

This enthusiastic election guide tried to breathe life into what for most Americans was a humdrum presidential campaign.

The Election of 1888

The presidential campaign was quiet and uneventful compared to the one four years earlier.

President Cleveland was too busy, he claimed, to campaign for a second term, a decision that may have contributed to his losing the election.

The central issue was the tariff. The Republicans were for a high tariff that would protect American business. The Democrats campaigned for a low tariff and retaining the gold standard. There was a minimum of mudslinging, although Cleveland's character was again unjustly attacked. Democratic agents called him The Beast of Buffalo and spread rumors that he had beaten his young wife while in a drunken rage. The rumors were completely baseless, but Frances was forced to issue a statement to finally quell them. She said that she wished "the women of our Country no greater blessing than that their homes and lives may be as happy, and their husbands may be as kind, considerate and affectionate as mine."

Cleveland refused to campaign and remained at work in the White House. Running mate Thurman was sent out on the campaign trail despite his poor health and advanced age. Harrison campaigned effectively from his front porch, receiving thousands of visitors and delivering hundreds of short speeches to them. Many leading Republicans campaigned for Harrison, including former presidential candidate James G. Blaine. Besides being well organized, the Republicans enjoyed a large war chest, made up of generous contributions mostly from wealthy businessmen. It was

JOSEPH JEFFERSON

The greatest comic actor of the nineteenth century was Joseph Jefferson, a good friend of President Cleveland. In a time before radio, film, and television, live theater was the main form of entertainment in American cities and towns. Actors such as Jefferson toured the country, performing in plays. His most famous role was playing Rip Van Winkle, the character from the Washington Irving story 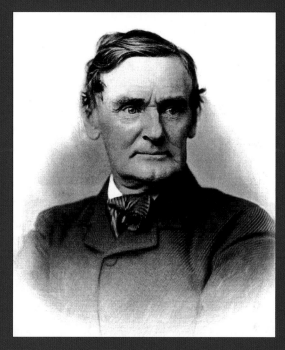 about a man who sleeps for twenty years. Jefferson performed the role for forty years. He was so great in the part that the public never tired of seeing him in it. In his younger days Jefferson played in actress Laura Keene's theater company. His first great role was opposite her in a comedy called *Our American Cousin*. Abraham Lincoln was watching Keene in a performance of this play on April 14, 1865, at Ford's Theatre in Washington, D.C., when he was assassinated by another actor, John Wilkes Booth. Jefferson died in 1905, a year after he retired from the stage. His name lives on in the annual Joseph Jefferson Awards, given to the best shows and actors in Chicago theater.

these factors that boosted Harrison to victory on November 6, Election Day. He decisively defeated Cleveland in the electoral college, 233 to 168. In the popular vote, however, Cleveland beat Harrison by about 100,000 votes, making it the closest presidential election up to that time.

Cleveland accepted defeat gracefully, almost gratefully. He claimed that there was "no happier man in the United States." He had no regrets about his stand on the tariff and other issues. "It is better to be defeated battling for an honest principle than to win by a cowardly subterfuge," he told a friend. But Frances predicted that he would be president again. "I want you to take good care of all the furniture and ornaments in the house," she told a White House servant before leaving the mansion, "for I want to find everything just as it is now, when we come back again. We are coming back, just four years from today."

A Quiet Life in New York

The Clevelands moved to New York City, where they rented a four-story brownstone on Madison Avenue near Sixty-eighth Street. The couple lived a relaxed and quiet life there. While he enjoyed playing the game of cribbage and going to the theater with his wife, Cleveland, now in his early fifties, was hardly ready for retirement. He joined the prestigious law firm of Bangs, Stetson, Tracy, and MacVeagh, where he did not practice law in the courts but was "of counsel."

In 1891 the couple bought a summer cottage on Cape Cod in Massachusetts near famed actor Joseph Jefferson and his wife. Jefferson and Cleveland were the best of friends and often fished together.

BABY RUTH

On October 3, 1891, Frances gave birth to a baby girl they named Ruth. A first-time father at fifty-four, Cleveland wrote to a friend that he felt as if "he had entered the real world."

The Cleveland's first child was the nation's darling when the family returned to the White House in 1893 (the same year, Frances gave birth to another daughter, Esther). The newspapers dubbed her Baby Ruth, and she was often seen playing on the

White House lawn. This ended when passersby began picking her up to play with her. After that Ruth was rarely seen in public, and rumors spread that the Cleveland's eldest daughter was deformed. At age twelve, Ruth contracted the disease diphtheria and died in 1904. Seventeen years later, the Curtiss Candy Company unveiled their Baby Ruth chocolate candy bar. They originally said it was named for the Clevelands' child, but that may not be true. Earlier, the company had tried to get baseball player Babe Ruth's endorsement for the bar. Many people believe they were really cashing in on Babe Ruth's popularity without having to pay him royalties. Baby Ruth is still a popular candy bar today and is manufactured by Nestlé.

While Cleveland fished and doted on his daughter, the Republicans were working hard at disassembling everything he had worked for during his presidency. The Republican Congress, with Harrison's support, raised the tariff to the highest it had ever been. Congress also passed the Sherman Silver Purchase Act, which increased the amount of silver currency, and passed a bill granting every Civil War veteran a pension. The Treasury surplus that Cleveland left dwindled to nothing as the Republican lawmakers spent recklessly, earning them the name the "Billion-Dollar Congress."

Early on in Harrison's administration, Cleveland, following a tradition of ex-presidents, offered no public criticism of his successor. But by 1891 Cleveland was speaking openly of the wasteful ways of the Republicans and giving speeches voicing his criticisms about once a month. "A condition of restlessness and irritation has grown up throughout the country," he told an audience at Tremont Temple in Boston on October 31, "born of prevailing inequality and unfairness, which threatens an attack upon sound currency, and which awakens the fear and anxious solicitude of thoughtful and patriotic men." By then it was clear Cleveland was positioning himself for another run for the White House.

THE ELECTION OF 1892

As the Democrats convened in Chicago in June 1892, Cleveland stood out as the most likely candidate with the strongest following. His main rival for the nomination was David B. Hill, his successor as governor of New York, who had the backing of Tammany Hall. But Hill's underhanded tactics at trying to tie up the New York delegation for himself was looked on unfavorably by most delegates, and Cleveland easily won the nomination on

CLEVELAND'S SECOND VICE PRESIDENT

Uncle Adlai, as he was known to his many friends and admirers, was a popular and affable politician and a good choice for Cleveland's running mate. He was born on October 23, 1835, on his family's farm in Christian County, Kentucky. Stevenson became a lawyer and served two terms in the U.S. House of Representatives before he was appointed first assistant postmaster general during Cleveland's first term. Stevenson earned the title The Headsman for axing 40,000 Republicans from the postal service rolls and replacing them with Democrats. After serving his term as vice president, Stevenson ran for the office again on the 1900 Democratic ticket with William Jennings Bryan, but Bryan lost to Republican William McKinley. Stevenson returned to his law practice in Illinois, where he ran for governor in 1908 and lost. Stevenson died on June 14, 1914. His grandson, Adlai Stevenson III, was the Democratic presidential candidate in 1952 and 1956, beaten both times by Republican Dwight D. Eisenhower. The younger Adlai inherited his grandfather's love of politics and his lively sense of humor.

the first ballot. Former Illinois congressman Adlai E. Stevenson was chosen as his running mate.

When the Republicans convened in Minneapolis, Minnesota, in June, some of them wanted to dump Harrison, who was not well liked by the public. But as the incumbent president, the majority of delegates decided to stick with him. Neither party seemed particularly enthusiastic about its candidates. Orator and author Robert Ingersoll noted, "Each side would have been glad to defeat the other if it could do so without electing its own candidate."

Looking suitably presidential, Cleveland campaigns for the third time for the highest office in the land in 1892.

Union members parade in Chicago in support of the Democratic ticket.

If there was any fire in the campaign, it came from a new third party, the People's, or Populist, Party. Made up mostly of farmers and urban workers, the Populist Party stood for an increase in silver currency, an eight-hour working day for laborers, and a one-term limit on presidents and vice presidents. They nominated Iowa lawyer James B. Weaver for president.

Neither Harrison nor Cleveland campaigned actively. When Harrison's first wife, Caroline, died of **tuberculosis** in October, he suspended his campaign briefly, as did Cleveland out of respect. As Election Day neared, many Americans were ready to return to the tougher but more stable policies of Grover Cleveland. He won the election handily: 277 electoral votes to Harrison's 145. Cleveland trounced Harrison in the popular vote, by more than 380,000 votes. Harrison failed to win even his home state of Indiana. Weaver and the Populists made a strong showing, winning 22 electoral votes and about a million popular votes.

Cleveland must have seen his victory as a vindication of sorts for his policies while president. He was ready to carry those policies forward in a second term. The Democrats were in a strong position to support him, having won majorities in both houses of Congress. That hadn't happened since 1856.

Most Americans seemed pleased to have Cleveland back in the White House, even the big industrialists who had not always seen eye to eye with him. "Cleveland! Landslide!" exclaimed steel magnate Andrew Carnegie. "Well, we have nothing to fear and perhaps it is best. . . . Cleveland is a pretty good fellow."

On the day of Grover Cleveland's second inauguration, March 4, 1893, Washington, D.C., was marred by by a blizzard. It was an omen of stormy times ahead. Delivering his inaugural address, again from memory, Cleveland stressed his commitment to fighting business monopolies, defending the rights of American Indians, and continuing the gold standard, to which he gave special emphasis. "It can not be doubted that our stupendous achievements as a people and our country's robust strength have given rise to heedlessness of those laws governing our national health which we can no more evade than human life can escape the laws of God and nature," he said. "Manifestly nothing is more vital to our supremacy as a nation and to the beneficent purposes of our

AGAIN ON DECK.

Executive-Officer CLEVELAND Reports for Duty on the SHIP OF STATE & is Warmly Welcomed.

"Thanks, Captain! Glad to get back and never better in my life."

REPEAL & REFORM

President Cleveland arrives for duty on the "ship of state" with a bag full of "Repeal and Reform" in this political cartoon. The bag may refer to the repeal of the Sherman Silver Purchase Act that many of Cleveland's supporters anticipated.

The new president reviews the grand procession in front of the White House on his second inauguration day.

An admission card to what was one of the grandest of inauguration days, and nights, up to that time.

Government than a sound and stable currency. Its exposure to degradation should at once arouse to activity the most enlightened statesmanship, and the danger of depreciation in the purchasing power of the wages paid to toil should furnish the strongest incentive to prompt and conservative precaution."

The inaugural ball that followed was one of the most spectacular to date. Incandescent lightbulbs, a new invention, spelled out the names of all previous presidents, while guests danced to the music of a 120-piece orchestra conducted by John Philip Sousa. When tired of dancing, the guests could dine on 60,000 oysters and 1,300 quarts of ice cream, among other delicacies.

The next day the new president was hard at work. To advise him, Cleveland picked another varied but strong cabinet. For secretary of state he chose Illinois's Walter Q. Gresham, who as a Republican had fought Harrison for the nomination four years earlier and switched parties in 1892 to support Cleveland. Richard B. Olney, a brilliant if hot-tempered administrator, became attorney general. Cleveland named his faithful friend Wilson Bissell postmaster general.

President Cleveland (far left) meets with his cabinet at the start of his second administration.

A Secret Operation

In May 1893, only two months into Cleveland's second term, the nation experienced an economic panic. Farm prices plummeted, and businesses failed. Many believed it was due largely to four years of Republican free spending under Harrison, which had dangerously depleted the gold reserves in the U.S. Treasury. In June Cleveland called a special session of Congress to convene in August "to the end that the people may be relieved through legislation from present and impending danger and distress." To accomplish this, Cleveland requested that Congress repeal the Sherman Silver Purchase Act, which he felt was largely responsible for flooding the market with silver and reducing the value of gold.

Depositors line up to get their money out of a bank during a financial panic. Such scenes became all too common as the economy faltered in the spring of 1893.

However, that same month the president experienced a personal crisis. On May 27, 1893, Cleveland discovered a rough patch on the roof of his mouth while brushing his teeth. White House doctor Robert M. O'Reilly examined the sore and determined it to be cancerous. A specialist was called in who told the president that the cancer should be removed immediately, before it could spread.

With the nation on the brink of a depression, Cleveland did not want his ill health to be the cause of more public unrest. The operation was conducted in complete secrecy, not in a hospital but aboard the yacht *Oneida* while it sailed up New York's East River and into Long Island Sound. Under these challenging conditions, the president was strapped into a chair tied to the boat's mast below decks. Five surgeons were present. The patient was given nitrous oxide, a new anesthetic, and a dentist extracted two teeth, giving the surgeons access to the infected area. The cancer proved to be more advanced than expected, and the surgeons had to cut out a large part of Cleveland's upper left jawbone and replaced it with a rubber **prosthesis**. The yacht sailed to Gray Gables, Cleveland's summer home on Cape Cod, where he recuperated and practiced speaking with the prosthesis. The president, fully recovered, returned to Washington in August and spoke before Congress without anyone suspecting the ordeal he had recently undergone. Congress repealed the Sherman Silver Purchase Act on October 30, 1893.

Cleveland's cancer operation remained a secret until 1917, nine years after his death, when one of the doctors who operated on him wrote an article about it for the *Saturday Evening Post* magazine.

With the Sherman Silver Purchase Act repealed, Cleveland was anxious to replace the Treasury's dwindling gold supply.

A King-size President

Cleveland's mouth cancer was probably the result of years of chewing tobacco and smoking cigars. But years of overeating created another health risk: obesity. By the time he first entered the White House in 1885, Cleveland weighed about 300 pounds, making him the second heaviest president, after William Howard Taft. While his weight did not interfere with his work habits in the White House, it did cramp his recreational activities. On a  vacation in the Adirondacks during his first term, the president couldn't keep up with his friends while hunting and restricted his activities to fishing and eating. Cleveland's taste in cuisine was basic. He disliked the French food served by the White House chef. Once when smelling the servants' dinner of corned beef and cabbage in the kitchen, he exchanged meals with them and later said it was the best dinner he'd had in months.

Cleveland's weight didn't seem to have bothered him much in the pretelevision era, when many successful men were grossly overweight. On one campaign trip he stopped in a small town, where he saw an elderly man staring at him.

"So you're the president," said the man.

"I am," replied Cleveland.

The man said Cleveland was the first president he'd ever saw.

"Well, what do you think?" Cleveland asked.

"You're a whopper," the man replied.

In 1895 he sold his old friend banker J. P. Morgan $600 million in U.S. bonds at a good rate for gold. The sale brought 3.5 million ounces of gold into the Treasury but cost the president much of the goodwill of the American people. Many of them saw his "gold deal" with Morgan as a sign that he favored big business and banks over the people's welfare. While it was true that Cleveland was no enemy of big business, the charge seems unfair. By bringing the gold into the Treasury so quickly, he saved the nation from further economic chaos and restored the financial reputation of the United States among the world's nations.

LABOR UNREST

Despite Cleveland's efforts, the depression continued into 1894, and American workers grew more unsatisfied with their domineering employers. Strikes took place across the country. One of the biggest was the Pullman strike in Chicago in May 1894. George Pullman, creator of the Pullman railroad car, ruled over his workers with an iron hand. The strike was led by Eugene V. Debs, the leader of the American Railway Union.

Attorney General Olney, who once was a lawyer for the railroads, was sympathetic to Pullman and pressured the reluctant president to issue an **injunction** to bring in federal troops to end the strike. Olney argued that the strike was interfering with the delivery of mail, a federal offense. This won over Cleveland, and he sent in the troops, warning the strikers with these words: "If it takes every dollar in the Treasury and every soldier in the United States to deliver a postal card in Chicago, that card should be delivered."

Rioting broke out in Chicago, the center of the strike, and troops moved in to quell it. In the ensuing violence twelve

Financier J. P. Morgan played a key role in restoring confidence to a failing economy, but Cleveland's dealings with him were criticized by many Americans.

people were killed and hundreds wounded. Debs, who didn't advocate violence, was arrested and sentenced to six months in jail. The strike ended, and many Americans approved of the way Cleveland handled it. Others, however, including Illinois governor John P. Altgeld, thought the government had overstepped its bounds. Forty years later a Supreme Court decision made it illegal for the government to issue an injunction against a strike.

Pullman strikers are fired upon by National Guardsmen in July 1894 in Chicago with the approval of Cleveland's Attorney General.

"Coxey's Army"

Shortly before the Pullman strike, Jacob Coxey, a concerned American businessman, led unemployed workers to Washington, D.C., to demonstrate against the government. Coxey left his home in Massillon, Ohio, on Easter Sunday 1894 with about 200 unemployed men. Coxey hoped to draw thousands of discontented workers into his "army," but at any time on the march it averaged only 250. Among these were newspaper men who daily reported on the progress of the march  in their newspapers. Coxey wanted to petition the government to issue $500 million in legal tender to fund a national road construction project that would put thousands of men back to work. On his arrival in Washington, D.C., he was arrested for trespassing on the Capitol lawn and never gave the speech he had prepared. He served twenty days in jail, and his army disbanded.

Despite his failure, Coxey lived to see his ideas for government aid to help the poor and unemployed become reality. President Franklin D. Roosevelt enacted such government legislation in the 1930s to fight the effects of the Great Depression (1929–1939). In 1944, on the fiftieth anniversary of his march, Coxey was invited to deliver his original speech on the steps of the Capitol.

Foreign Affairs

The nineteenth century was a time of empire building for the European powers. They colonized many countries and peoples in Africa, Asia, and Latin America. As the century was drawing to a close, many Americans felt it was time for the United States, emerging as a world power, to establish colonies and build its own empire. President Cleveland, who felt America should be a beacon of freedom for all nations, didn't agree. His beliefs were put to the test in 1893. That year American planters and businessmen who lived and worked in the Hawaiian Islands supported the overthrow of Queen Liliuokalani, Hawaii's monarch. They established a provisional government under Samuel B. Dole, an American landowner and businessman. Dole appealed to Cleveland to **annex** the Hawaiian Islands in the name of the United States.

Cleveland refused. In his annual message on December 2, 1893, he said that "it seemed to me the only honorable course for our government to pursue was to undo the wrong that had been done by those representing us and to restore as far as practicable the status at the time of our forcible intervention." But to do that was difficult. Not wanting to force out Americans who had been in Hawaii for years, Cleveland stopped short of restoring the queen to power. In 1898, during the administration of Republican president William McKinley, Hawaii was officially annexed by order of Congress. Hawaii remained a U.S. territory until it became the fiftieth state in 1959.

In 1895 Walter Gresham died, and Richard Olney became secretary of state. One of the first issues with which Olney had to deal was a long-running border dispute between the British

QUEEN LILIUOKALANI, HAWAII'S LAST MONARCH

When Liliu Kamakaeha ascended to the Hawaiian throne as Queen Liliuokalani following the death of her brother King David Kalakaua in 1891, American interests in Hawaii were pleased. They felt she would be as compliant to their needs as her late brother had been. But the new queen proved strong willed and disdainful of the American intruders. She revoked an 1887 constitution that gave rights to foreigners, and she limited the vote to native Hawaiians.

The Americans, who wanted more land and resources, staged a revolt and deposed Queen Lil, as she was called. When Hawaii was annexed by the United States in 1898, the queen was given a small pension for life. She made two trips to the United States and remained a popular figure among her people until her death in 1917. She is best remembered today as the composer of the song "Aloha Oe," which has become the traditional farewell song of Hawaii.

colony of Guyana and Venezuela in South America. Cleveland had attempted unsuccessfully to work out an arbitration for the dispute in his first term. In July 1895 Olney responded to another rebuff from Britain with a sharply worded note, vowing that if the British tried to take the disputed territory from Venezuela by force, the United States would intervene under the guidelines of the **Monroe Doctrine**. Established in 1825, this doctrine declared that any interference by a European nation in an independent country in the Americas would be viewed as an unfriendly act dangerous to peace and would be treated as such by the United States.

Uncle Sam stands ready to defend Venezuela from the European powers in this political cartoon that approves of Cleveland's actions in the border dispute.

The British responded that their claim on the border region predated the existence of Venezuela and did not fall under the Monroe Doctrine. Cleveland, who thought Olney might have gone too far, was incensed by this reply and said that if Great Britain did not agree to arbitration, the United States would step in to protect Venezuela. Tension built for weeks, and then the British backed down. The claim was peacefully arbitrated in 1899.

As his second term was drawing to a close, Cleveland had continued to show strength and courage in dealing with domestic and international matters, even if he wasn't always on the winning side. But more and more he was finding himself out of step with a younger generation of politicians who wanted to see America exercise its power abroad and go from an economy built on the gold standard to one built on cheap and plentiful free silver.

Democratic presidential candidate William Jennings Bryan rides to center stage of the convention on a silver coin in this political cartoon. Bryan's advocacy of free silver went directly against Cleveland's support of the gold standard.

THE SAGE OF PRINCETON

$\mathcal{G}$rover Cleveland had started his second term a popular president. He ended it highly unpopular, with his own party deserting him and his policies. Cleveland did not expect, and probably did not seek, to run for a third term; but as president, he wanted some respect from the Democrats at their convention in Chicago in June 1896. Instead, he was vilified by South Carolina governor "Pitchfork Ben" Tillman as "a tool of Wall Street." Such an attack at a convention on a sitting president by a member of his own party was unprecedented.

Perhaps worse, the man who won the Democratic presidential nomination opposed nearly everything for which Cleveland stood. Thirty-six-year-old William Jennings Bryan was a former congressman from Nebraska and a strong advocate for the common man and the use of free silver to solve the country's economic problems. A brilliant orator, Bryan delivered a speech before the convention that ended with these words: "You shall not press down upon the brow of labor this crown of thorns, you shall not crucify mankind upon a cross of gold." The "Cross of Gold" speech mesmerized the delegates and helped Bryan gain the nomination for president on the fifth ballot. Arthur Sewall, a banker from Maine, was nominated as his running mate.

A number of so-called Bourbon Democrats favored the gold standard that Cleveland supported. They were aghast at Bryan's nomination and in September formed their own splinter party: the National Democratic, or Sound Money, Party. They asked

Cleveland to run for a third term as their candidate, but he refused. He was probably tired of being president and didn't see how he could win the election. The Sound Money Party instead chose Illinois senator John M. Palmer as their candidate. Cleveland endorsed Palmer but played no role in the campaign.

THE ELECTION OF 1896

Three weeks before the Democratic convention, the Republicans met and nominated two-time governor of Ohio William McKinley for president. Cleveland knew McKinley well and liked him. McKinley greatly admired Cleveland and had visited him in the White House.

While Bryan crisscrossed the country, Republican candidate William McKinley campaigned from his front porch in Canton, Ohio.

The fall campaign was a lively one, mostly due to Bryan's energy and enthusiasm. Unlike most presidential candidates up to that time, he did not sit back and let others campaign for him. He crossed the country, giving up to six speeches a day. McKinley, in contrast, never left his front porch in Ohio, giving speeches to large groups of visitors from there. He was the first presidential candidate to make extensive use of that recent invention the telephone in his campaign.

Cleveland seems happy and content to be retired from the presidency in this 1899 portrait.

Backed by Ohio industrialist Mark Hanna, McKinley had a large war chest of money to spend. On Election Day he beat Bryan decisively: 271 to 176 electoral votes. The popular vote was: McKinley 7,102,246 and Bryan 6,492,559. Cleveland was delighted with the results. While McKinley had wisely played both sides of the gold-silver question, Cleveland knew he stood for sound money and a continuation of the gold standard.

Cleveland gave his last state of the union message on December 7, 1896. He said in closing:

In concluding this communication its last words shall be an appeal to the Congress for the most rigid economy in the expenditure of the money it holds in trust for the people. The way to perplexing extravagance is easy, but a return to frugality is difficult. When, however, it is considered that those who bear the burdens of taxation have no guaranty of honest care save in the fidelity of their public servants, the duty of all possible retrenchment is plainly manifest. When our differences are forgotten and our contests of political opinion are no longer remembered, nothing in the retrospect of our public service will be as fortunate and comforting as the recollection of official duty well performed and the memory of a constant devotion to the interests of our confiding fellow-countrymen.

MOVING TO PRINCETON

Cleveland watched the inauguration of McKinley on March 4, 1897, with bittersweet feelings. "I envy him today only one thing and that was the presence of his own mother at the inauguration," he said later. "I would have given anything in the world if my mother could have been at my inauguration." The Clevelands left Washington with no intention of ever returning. They settled in Princeton, New Jersey, home of prestigious Princeton University. Grover and Frances had visited Princeton earlier and been greatly impressed by its natural beauty and quietude, a far cry from the frantic pace of Washington. They moved into a colonial mansion not far from the campus, which they named Westland in honor of classics professor Andrew Fleming West, who had encouraged and helped them in their move to Princeton.

The stately buildings and peaceful atmosphere of Princeton University held great appeal for Cleveland and his wife who moved here in 1897.

Cleveland vs. Wilson

On June 2, 1902, Woodrow Wilson, a professor of jurisprudence and political economy, was elected president of Princeton by the trustees. Cleveland liked Wilson's innovative ideas and dynamic leadership, and the two man became friends. When he heard Wilson recite the poem "Chant of the Happy Warrior" by William Wordsworth, it became Cleveland's favorite poem.

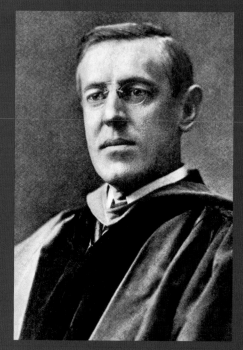

However, when Wilson clashed with Andrew West, dean of the graduate school, over the location of the new graduate school, Cleveland sided with his old friend West. Wilson and Cleveland's relationship was never the same after that. Yet when Cleveland died in 1908, Wilson spoke with generous praise of the ex-president. "He did much more than give the prestige of his great name to the university: he served it with thoughtful intelligence and conscientious devotion," wrote Wilson.

Wilson resigned from Princeton two years later and was elected governor of New Jersey. In a whirlwind political rise as rapid as Cleveland's, he was nominated for president by the Democrats in 1912 and won the election. Wilson and Cleveland were the only Democrats to serve as president from the Civil War to the Great Depression of the 1930s.

The Princeton community was greatly honored to have an ex-president in their midst. Cleveland, who never went to college, was flattered by the attention and dived into university affairs with characteristic vigor. At first he was mostly a figurehead, marching in graduation exercises at the head alongside the university president. However, soon he was asked to preside over Princeton-Yale debates and, beginning in 1899, was invited to lecture once or twice a year on topics of his choosing, mostly about events from his presi-

Cleveland, who never attended college, delighted in participating in the pomp of Princeton graduations and other ceremonial occasions.

dency. In 1903 he was named a trustee of the university. The newspapers were calling him "the Sage of Princeton." After his death, the university dedicated the 173-foot Cleveland Tower on the grounds of the Princeton graduate school in his honor.

AUTHOR AND EX-PRESIDENT

Cleveland was fifty-nine years old when he left the presidency, and he enjoyed living in retirement with his young wife and children, who then numbered five. Richard was born in 1897 and Francis in 1903. The joy of Francis's birth was soon marred by the death of the Clevelands' eldest daughter, Ruth, the following year. The blow was a hard one, and Cleveland plunged into work to try to forget his loss.

He had enjoyed writing two books earlier in his life and returned to writing. *Presidential Problems*, a collection of his lectures, appeared in 1904, followed by *Fishing* and *Good Hunting Sketches* (1906) and *Good Citizenship* (1908). He also wrote numerous articles and features for magazines ranging from *The*

Proud parents pose with their four children in 1907. The ex-president would be dead within the next year.

The Muckrackers

While Cleveland was writing for the magazines, so were a new group of journalists who attacked vice and corruption in American cities in their articles. In a speech in 1906 President Theodore Roosevelt labeled them "muckrakers." The first successful muckraker was Lincoln Steffens, who wrote a detailed exposé of political corruption in St. Louis, Missouri, in *McClure's Magazine* in 1903. Steffens later collected his magazine exposés into a groundbreaking book, *Shame of the Cities*. Another prominent muckraker was Ida M. Tarbell, whose *History of the Standard Oil Company* exposed the sins of big business and was first serialized in *McClure's*. Upton Sinclair brought muckraking into fiction with his fact-based novel *The Jungle* (1906), a shocking exposé of unsanitary conditions in the stockyards and meatpacking companies of Chicago. The novel became a best seller and led Congress to pass the first of the Pure Food and Drug Acts later that same year. The muckrakers helped to usher in the Progressive era of political and social reform in America, but their day passed by 1912 due to a growing sensationalism in their writing.

Saturday Evening Post to *Ladies' Home Journal*. He was well paid for his writing. That, together with the income he'd saved from his salary as president, allowed the Clevelands to live comfortably, if not luxuriously.

While Cleveland defended his presidency in print, he was pleased to see that people were beginning to look favorably on his two administrations again. With the death of Benjamin Harrison in March 1901 and the tragic assassination of President McKinley

The St. Louis World's Fair

By 1904 world's fairs were becoming common in America, showcasing the city in which each was held and displaying new technologies and ideas. The St. Louis fair was held to commemorate the Louisiana Purchase of 1804, which doubled the size of the United States. The fair was held in the city's Forest Park, which the same year was the site of the first Olympic Games to be held in America. Nearly 20 million visitors from the United States and abroad flocked to St. Louis to see highlights of the fair, such as an automobile that had driven all the way from New York City. They could taste new treats such as the ice cream cone and drink a new beverage: iced tea. They could listen to a band play the new song sensation written specially for the fair, "Meet Me in St. Louis," a song that is still popular today.

the following September in Buffalo, Cleveland was the only living former president. As such, he was invited to appear at the 1904 Louisiana Purchase Exposition in St. Louis, Missouri, with President Theodore Roosevelt, who succeeded McKinley.

At the Democratic presidential convention in July of that year, some newspapers suggested that Cleveland be drafted to run for a third term. Few, including Cleveland himself, took the suggestion seriously. The Democrats ended up nominating Alton B. Parker, chief justice of the New York State Supreme Court, as their candidate. Parker was a Bourbon Democrat who supported fiscal conservatism, as Cleveland did. The former president campaigned actively for Alton and was surprised and disappointed when he lost to Roosevelt in the November election.

Last Days

In 1905 Cleveland accepted an appointment as a trustee of the Equitable Life Assurance Society. He was no figurehead but took a central role in reorganizing the company, which was riddled with waste and corruption. He did such a good job in restoring confidence in the company that in 1907 he was named leader of the Association of Presidents of Life Insurances Companies.

On his seventieth birthday Cleveland was presented with a silver loving cup by the students of Princeton. "I feel young at seventy," he said with deep emotion, "because I have here breathed the atmosphere of vigorous youth."

But the ills of old age were closing in on him. He suffered from heart and kidney disease and by April 1908 was bedridden. The end came on June 24, 1908, when Cleveland suffered a fatal heart attack. His last recorded words were "I have tried so hard to do right." Cleveland's funeral, as he wished, was a simple affair

This late portrait shows an aged and ailing Cleveland.

attended by President Roosevelt and a small group of friends and politicians. He was buried in the family plot in Princeton Cemetery alongside his daughter Ruth. In a proclamation on his death, Roosevelt wrote that Cleveland "showed signal powers as an administrator, coupled with entire devotion to the country's good, and a courage that quailed before no hostility when once he was convinced where his duty lay."

LEGACY

"Grover the Good" is a fitting epithet for a president who always tried to do his best. His intentions were good, his honesty was unquestioned for the most part, and his courage to take a stand for what he believed in, regardless of the consequences, was unwavering. Contemporary historians rank him as the best president we had between Lincoln and Theodore Roosevelt. Unfortunately, he is better remembered for his two nonconsecutive terms than for any of his achievements. And there were some important ones. He restored integrity and honesty to the White House at a time when corruption and graft in politics was the norm. He supported the gold standard at a time when to abandon it would have plunged the country into greater economic chaos.

Even some of Cleveland's failures can be seen as successes in the long run. He was unable to reduce the high tariffs on imported goods, but his ceaseless struggle against them eventually led to their lowering and to the flowering of free trade with other countries. In foreign affairs his refusal to annex Hawaii was overturned in the next administration. However, his strong moral stand against American imperialism resonated and kept America from becoming a colonial power, despite the temporary possession of Cuba and the Philippines after the Spanish-American War of 1898.

Cleveland had his faults, and they may have prevented this good president from achieving greatness. His view of the president as a naysayer or gatekeeper and not an activist limited his accomplishments. He refused to use federal power and money to help the needy, such as the drought-stricken farmers of Texas, in his first term. But these faults were not peculiar to Cleveland's presidency. They were part of a mind-set that pervaded American society in the post–Civil War era and beyond. Not until Franklin Roosevelt's New Deal did the federal government offer widespread aid to those Americans in need.

On balance, Cleveland was the best president he could be for his time and within his limitations. His qualities of courage, honesty, and hard work are those that every great leader should have. As his biographer Henry Graff has written, "[H]e exuded sincerity and decency. No one ever doubted what he meant or where he stood." Or as historian Alan Nevis put it, "It is as a strong man, a man of character, that Cleveland will live in history."

Honest, hard-working, and just, Grover Cleveland has been judged by historians as perhaps the best president of the post-Civil War era.

1837
Born March 18 in Caldwell, New Jersey

1859
Becomes a lawyer in Buffalo, New York

1870
Elected sheriff of Erie County, New York

1881
Elected mayor of Buffalo

1882
Elected governor of New York State

1884
Elected twenty-second president of the United States

1830

1886

Marries Frances Folsom in the White House

1888

Loses reelection to Benjamin Harrison

1892

Elected twenty-fourth president of the United States

1897

Leaves Washington, D.C., at end of his second term and settles in Princeton, New Jersey

1908

Dies at his home in Princeton, on June 24

1910

NOTES

CHAPTER ONE

p.9, "Often and often as a boy . . ." Grover Cleveland, quoted in Henry F. Graff,
Grover Cleveland. New York: Henry Holt and Company, 2002, p. 8.

p.11, "They have gone with me . . ." Grover Cleveland, quoted in Graff, p. 9.

p.18, "[a] few Buffalo people still live . . ." *The New York Times*, July 7, 1912.

CHAPTER TWO

p.21, "I regard it as the culmination . . ." Grover Cleveland, quoted in Zachary Kent,
Grover Cleveland. Chicago, Il: Children's Press, 1988, p. 33.

p.23, "Good and pure government lies . . ." Grover Cleveland, quoted in Graff, p. 20.

p.24, "The intentions now transferred . . ." Grover Cleveland, quoted in Graff, p. 32.

p.31, "Women now married and anxious . . ." quoted in Graff, p. 62.

p.31, "Tell the truth." Grover Cleveland, quoted in Graff, p. 62.

p.31, "Ma, ma, where's my Pa? . . ." David C. Whitney and Robin Vaughn Whitney, *The
American Presidents*. Pleasantville, NY: Reader's Digest Association, 1996, p. 179.

p.34, "Blaine! Blaine! James G. Blaine!" Whitney and Whitney, p. 178.

p.35, "We are Republicans . . ." Samuel D. Burchard, quoted in Paul F. Boller, Jr.,
Presidential Campaigns. New York: Oxford University Press, 1984, p. 149.

p.35, "Hurrah for Maria! . . ." Boller, Jr., p. 151.

CHAPTER THREE

p.37, "To-day the executive branch . . ." Grover Cleveland, First Inaugural Address.
www.bartleby.com/124/pres37.html (Accessed June 10, 2009).

p.39, "My God, what is there . . ." Grover Cleveland, quoted in Graff, p. 82.

p.40, "May God palsy the hand . . ." Lucius Fairchild, quoted in Graff, p. 84.

p.40, "Though the people support . . ." Graff, p. 85.

p.41, "Federal aid in such cases . . ." The Official White House Website.www.white-
house.gov/history/presidents/gc2224.html (Accessed January 16, 2009).

p.47, "I was waiting . . ." Grover Cleveland, quoted in Sid Frank and Arden Davis Melick,
The Presidents: Tidbits and Trivia. Maplewood, N.J.: Hammond, Inc., 1980, p. 6.

p.48, "My mother did not want . . ." Marion Cleveland, quoted in Carl Sferrazza
Anthony, *America's First Families*. New York: Touchstone Books, 2000, p. 309.

p.50, "What do you think the American people . . ." Grover Cleveland, quoted in Graff, *Grover Cleveland*, p. 75.

p.52, "a stream of light should pierce . . ." Grover Cleveland, quoted in Leslie Allen, *Liberty: The Statue and the American Dream*. New York: The Statue of Liberty-Ellis Island Foundation, 1985, p. 36.

CHAPTER FOUR

p.55, "Kid Glove." Boller, Jr., p. 58.

p.56, "the women of our Country . . ." Frances Cleveland, quoted in Boller, Jr., p. 158.

p.58, "no happier man . . ." Grover Cleveland, quoted in Whitney and Whitney, p. 181.

p.58, "It is better to be . . ." Grover Cleveland, quoted in Boller, Jr., p. 159.

p.58, "I want you to take good care . . ." Frances Cleveland, quoted in Graff, p. 97.

p.59, "he had entered the real world." quoted in Graff, Grover Cleveland, p. 100.

p.60, "Billion-Dollar Congress." Whitney and Whitney, The American President, p. 182.

p.60, "A condition of restlessness and irritation . . ." Grover Cleveland, quoted in Graff, p. 105.

p.62, "Each side would have been glad . . ." Robert Ingersoll, quoted in Boller, Jr., p. 162.

p.64, "Cleveland! Landslide!" Andrew Carnegie, quoted in Boller, Jr., p. 165.

CHAPTER FIVE

p.65, "It can not be doubted . . ." Grover Cleveland–Second Inaugural Address. www.bartleby.com/124/pres39.html (Accessed June 10, 2009).

p.68, "to the end that the people may be . . ." Grover Cleveland, quoted in Whitney and Whitney, *The American Presidents*, p. 183.

p.71, "So you're the president . . ." Frank and Melick, p. 21.

p.72, "If it takes every dollar . . ." Grover Cleveland, quoted in Graff, p. 119.

p.76, "it seemed to me the only honorable course . . ." Grover Cleveland, quoted in Graff, pp. 122–123.

CHAPTER SIX

p.81, "a tool of Wall Street." Benjamin Tillman, quoted in Graff, p. 127.

p.81, "You shall not press down upon . . ." William Jennings Bryan, quoted in Graff, p. 128.

p.84, "In concluding this communication . . ." Grover Cleveland–Fourth Annual Message. The American Presidential Project. www.presidency.ucsb.edu/ws/index.php?pid=29537 (Accessed June 10, 2009).

p.84, "I envy him today only one thing . . ." Grover Cleveland, quoted in Whitney and Whitney, p. 187.

p.86, 'He did much more than give . . ." Woodrow Wilson, quoted in Princeton.edu (Accessed June 10, 2009).

p.87, "the Sage of Princeton." Graff, p. 131.

p.91, "I feel young at seventy . . ." Grover Cleveland, quoted in Princeton.edu (Accessed June 10, 2009).

p.91, "I have tried so hard . . ." Grover Cleveland, quoted in Graff, p. 135.

p.93, "showed signal powers as an administrator . . ." Theodore Roosevelt, quoted in *The New York Times*, June 25, 1908, p. 1.

p.94, "[H]e exuded sincerity and decency. . . ." Graff, p. 137.

p.110, "It is as a strong man . . ." Encyclopedia Americana Online (Accessed June 10, 2009).

GLOSSARY

abolition the movement to end slavery in the United States

anarchists persons who seek to overturn a government and its institutions by means of violence

annex to incorporate territory into a city, state, or country

ballot a vote, especially one to choose nominees at a political convention

brevet a commission of a military officer to a higher rank, often temporary, without an increase of pay

bustle a projecting framework once worn under the back of a woman's dress

confederacy an alliance of states for some purpose

dark horse a candidate who is unexpectedly nominated at a political convention

draft a selection of persons for military service, usually during wartime

Democratic Party one of America's two major political parties, founded in 1828

electoral vote vote cast during national presidential elections by specially chosen representatives from each state who form the electoral college; electoral votes, not popular votes, decide presidential elections

graft the acquiring of money dishonestly through political influence or power

impeachment the act of formally accusing a public official of misconduct in office and putting that individual on trial

incumbent currently holding a public office

injunction a judicial order prohibiting a person or group of persons from doing something, such as going on strike

joiner a carpenter who builds doors and windows

kickback a portion of funds given underhandedly to a politician for making the funding possible

Monroe Doctrine a doctrine adapted by the United States in 1823 that opposed further European colonization or intervention in the Americas

Mugwumps Republicans who refused to support presidential nominee James G. Blaine in the campaign of 1884

popular vote the actual total number of votes cast in national presidential elections by the voters

prosthesis an artificial device that replaces a missing part of the body

Quaker a member of a Christian religious denomination that believes in peace and opposes all wars

Republican Party one of America's two major political parties, founded in 1854

seceded broke away from an alliance or federation, such as the Southern states from the United States during the late 1800s

suffragettes women who advocated voting rights for women

tariff a duty imposed on goods, often ones coming from another country

tuberculosis a bacterial disease that often attacks the respiratory system

veto to turn down a bill passed by Congress before it becomes law

ward a political district of a town or city

Further Information

Books

Gaines, Ann. *Grover Cleveland: Our Twenty-Second and Twenty-Fourth President* (Presidents of the U.S.A.). Mankato, MN: Child's World, 2008.

Markel, Rita J. *Grover Cleveland* (Presidential Leaders). Minneapolis, MN: Lerner Publishing Group, 2006.

Ochester, Betsy. *Grover Cleveland: America's 22nd and 24th President* (Encyclopedia of Presidents, Second Series). Danbury, CT: Children's Press, 2004.

Venezia, Mike. *Grover Cleveland* (Getting to Know the U.S. Presidents). Danbury, CT: Children's Press, 2006.

Williams, Jean Kinney. *Grover Cleveland* (Profiles of the Presidents). Mankato, MN: Compass Point Books, 2003.

DVD

The American President. PBS Home Video, boxed DVD set, 2000.

WEBSITES

American President: An Online Reference Resource

www.millercenter.virginia.edu/academic/americanpresident/cleveland

This informative site includes short, concise biographies of not only Cleveland but also of his wife, vice presidents, and all the members of his two cabinets.

American Presidents

www.americanpresidents.org/presidents/22.asp

This statistical profile includes a list of Cleveland historic sites and a detailed bibliography.

Museum of History: Hall of U.S. Presidents

grovercleveland.org

This site includes a portrait of Cleveland, a brief biography, and a letter written by him after leaving the presidency.

The White House

www.whitehouse.gov/about/presidents/grovercleveland/22

The White House website features Cleveland's story as part of the ongoing tale of American presidents, from George Washington to Barack Obama.

★ ★ ★ ★ ★ ★ ★ ★ ★ ★ ★ ★ ★ ★ ★ ★ ★ ★ ★

BIBLIOGRAPHY

Allen, Leslie. *Liberty: The Statue and the American Dream.* New York: The Statue of Liberty-Ellis Island Foundation, 1985.

Anthony, Carl Sferrazza. *America's First Families.* New York: Touchstone Books, 2000.

Boller, Paul F., Jr. *Presidential Campaigns.* New York: Oxford University Press, 1984.

Frank, Sid, and Arden Davis Melick. *The Presidents: Tidbits and Trivia.* Maplewood, NJ: Hammond, Inc., 1980.

Graff, Henry F. *Grover Cleveland.* New York: Henry Holt & Company, 2002.

Kent, Zachary. *Grover Cleveland* (Encyclopedia of Presidents). Chicago, Il: Children's Press, 1988.

Paletta, Lee Ann. *The World Almanac of First Ladies.* New York: Pharos Books, 1990.

——, and Fred Worth. *The World Almanac Book of Presidential Facts.* New York: Pharos Books, 1988.

Whitney, David C., and Robin Vaughn Whitney. *The American Presidents.* Pleasantville, NY: Reader's Digest Association, 1996.

INDEX

Pages in **boldface** are illustrations.

ABOUT THE AUTHOR

Steven Otfinoski is the author of more than 135 children's titles. He previously wrote *Calvin Coolidge* and *Chester Arthur* for Marshall Cavendish's Presidents and Their Times and is working on two more biographies in this series. Otfinoski lives in Connecticut with his wife, Beverly, an editor and English teacher.

★ ★ ★ ★ ★ ★ ★ ★ ★ ★ ★ ★ ★ ★ ★ ★ ★ ★